BE PREPARED TO BE LUMINOUS

ROSALEEN CROWLEY

ISBN: 979-8-218-31394-4
Typesetting and cover design by Nick Sanquest
Printed by KDP
First published 2023
©Roscro and Co, LLC
Art by Roscro
Also by Rosaleen Crowley: *Point of Connection*, *Point of Reflection*, *Point of Perception*, *For the Sake of Rhyme*, and *Of Land and Poetry: Ireland*
Website: roscro.wordpress.com

To Sophie Jane Crowley,
my granddaughter

*What an amazing journey beckons
Loving parents will show you the light.*
from 'Sophie Jane From Nana'

About the Author

A graduate of University College Cork, Ireland, Rosaleen Crowley works as a poet, artist and educator. She is owner of Roscro and Co, LLC.

She enjoys her volunteer positions as Co-Founder/President of Carmel Creative Writers, Inc. and Interest Group Leader for the writing group of International Women Indiana.

Rosaleen lives in Zionsville, Indiana, USA.

Preface

Please enjoy this compilation of poems. I hope they take you on an exploration of yourself from beginnings to new beginnings and even startovers and back to being grounded in acceptance of one's self.

The new poems added to those already published poems in my trilogy show a progression and each section explores further the concepts of connection, reflection and perception.

I hope my poems inspire you to be your best. Most of all, be kind and take care of your loved ones. They deserve to be put first while you work on your luminosity.

Rosaleen

Contents

i: surroundings

Spring – Start Over	1
A Taste of Indiana	2
A Piece of Land of My Own	3
The Beauty of Naïveté	4
Planting Pansies	5
Between the Trees, Along the Path	6
The Willow Trees	7
On Walking Schoen Creek Trail	8
Moving to the Country	9
Love Lives Here	10
Barn Door	12
Loving Where I Am Planted	13
Zionsville: A Sense of Place	14

ii: people

Little Girl	17
Patchwork Quilter	18
Wedding Day	19
Aubrey Lynn from Nana	20
Harper Katherine from Nana	21
Chloe Elizabeth from Nana	22
Sophie Jane From Nana	23
Very Proud Nana	24
Reflection of a Perfect Visit	25
On Seeing A Woman's Side Profile	26
Hands	27

iii: gratitude

A Moment in Time	29
Gratitude for Life and Love	30
Lessons in Life	31
Passage of Time	32
Thank you, Grandma	33

iv: contemplation

Simple Rejection	35
Another Rejection	36
Café Life	37
Waiting	38
writing	39
Glass Paperweight	40
You Are Your Own Kite	41
Words Come in Dreams	42
Through the Window	43
Before the Rain and Then	44
Hand Written Letter	45
The Torn Letter	46
Hanging Pear	47
Red Bowl	48
She Gave Me Courage	49
Let Prayer Win – Looking for a Miracle	50
Eames Table and Chair	51
Finding Purple	52
Lessons From Your Best Self	53
Once Again	54
With Purple in Sight	55
Dancing Flowers	56

i

surroundings

Spring – Start Over

Remember last year's Spring,
Yellow daffodils in a mass,
Birds flew home on the wing,
Rabbits chased across grass.

Same today, seasons bring
Seasonal mixed weather,
Life begins again, floating
Softly like a feather.

Upbeat, important to note
Life can only get better,
Not worse, we can always hope.
Let's write a letter.

"Dear self," open your heart,
Stop keeping score,
Every day, do your part
To love more and more.

Step up to the challenge,
Communicate and follow through,
Read, walk, do not avenge
The toxicity of those you knew.

Next year, look back and say
You are nearer to the prize,
Simple steps day by day,
Remember, time flies.

And so, another year will come and go,
Success measured in friendships and love,
Be prepared to be luminous and glow
Like a lightbulb shining from above.

A Taste of Indiana

On arriving in Indiana, my new American destination
Over thirty years ago, the road led me south
To Bloomington, Lake Monroe and Madison.

Water and hills were the attraction.
Along byways and highways, through ups and downs,
What followed was exploration.

Seeking peace and connectivity,
Nature is powerful, the images transform
And pull you in and let you go on your way happily.

Next, taking a northern direction
Shipshewana, the land of Amish
Quilts and organic food, a wondrous selection.

A slower pace, a country feel,
It's all in the detail, horse drawn buggies
Connected by a big wooden, hand-made wheel.

Going west, just for the day to covered bridges,
Following a map, people waving from their porch.
Waterfalls and winding roads across fields and ridges.

Festivals and friendliness,
Visitors and locals
Experienced a time of togetherness.

To take in the home of Poet Riley
I traveled to Greencastle
A band of poets read original poems heartily.

Reading in front of an audience
Brings joy to each moment,
My life making sense.

And so whether North, South, East or West
From start to finish
Indiana continues to offer its best.

A Piece of Land of My Own

This time the house sits close to the road,
People wave as they go by,
Some stop but have to move due to traffic.

The postal worker walks to the front door.
You can hear her talking on her phone
Before you hear the plop of the mail.

The yard (or garden,
If you use European vernacular)
Is small but manicured.

Hydrangeas need help,
Maple trees are being treated
To save them from disease.

My favorite feature is the boxwoods,
Straight, tidy, strong,
Giving me a feeling of being protected.

Summer brings foliage to hide other backyards,
Winter allows depth of view.
Each season brings its own advantage.

Spring brings buds and birds,
Fall (or Autumn if you use European vernacular)
Brings bursts of colors, reds and purples.

Whichever way you look at it,
My land in Indiana is home.
I feel lucky to be alive.

The Beauty of Naïveté

From blank canvas to paradise
This painting reminds me
Of a line in one of my poems,
'Winter allows depth of view'

It started with a need for a balcony
To sit and take in the view,
A breezeway where two chairs
Can sit facing the view.

I took it upon myself through imagination
To be able to see the view before me
Every day whether Summer, Winter, Spring or Fall.
Paints, brushes and canvas were needed.

I've learned to love the imperfect.
I've learned to believe in my point of view
I'm lucky to believe
That my natural talent is enough.

I don't need to impress,
I don't need to stress
I don't need to define my success
By other people's acceptance.

I am curious if anyone sees what I see
I am curious to learn
If this excites any one besides me?
In the end, I've experienced the view.

I made it my own
I made a revelation
Life is good
Life is for living.
This scene is now recorded for posterity.

You can bring something alive
From blank canvas to paradise.
An Indiana paradise.

Planting Pansies

The blue pansies looked frail
When I chose them at the store.
I put them into pots
Divided by four.

My neighbor came and gave me topsoil,
He taught me how to separate them
And told me they needed water
To grow and blossom.

I'm glad to say all is well
I only once did have to spray
The petals and the roots
Because it rained most every day.

Now, how long will they last?
A week, a month, a season?
They have more chance than before
Since I have learned a lesson.

Choose wisely, listen to good counsel,
Respect the earth and do your part
To nurture, protect and
Love what you do with your heart.

When you take care of nature
The karma will come back to you.
A peaceful life, a purposeful life
Awaits and fills you with joy anew.

Just like the pansies needed water
In order to blossom, we need love and laughter.

Between the Trees, Along the Path
Monon Trail, Carmel Indiana

Between the trees, along the path
I hear the woodpecker tap, tap, tap.
Beneath the bridge, cyclists roll through
Pedaling and laughing two by two.

Friends holding hands, walkers with dogs,
A spring in their step, the jogger jogs,
On and on with strolling feet
Hoping I'll find some friends to greet.

A nod, a smile, a wave motion
Leads to a silent reflection.
Energy lost and now gained
I'm so glad it hasn't rained.

The Willow Trees
Holcomb Gardens, Butler University

From where the willows stand
Drooping, like water spraying from a faucet,
The dusty road looks comforting.
Fresh, like raindrops falling to the ground
I sit still
My presence observed and felt.

Across the bridge
The path turns and twists
The water is strewn with leaves
Dead, like bait bobbing on a line.

Back again to the row of willows
I stand beneath,
Protected from the elements
Pushed and pulled, my consciousness connects
I'm released from my dream
One being, one nature, one poem.

On waking from a dream
"The willow tree will be in the first round."

On Walking in Schoen Creek Trail
Fort Harrison State Park

What makes us wander through the woods?
The smells, the sounds, the many hues,
The hope of seasons' berry foods
Or catching the poetic muse?

Like mix of flour and milk for dough
Together, pummeled and smoothed,
Words and phrases flourish and flow
Reminds me of a lover wooed.

Journey similar to this poem,
Hearts and spirits rooted indeed,
Tall sycamore more than its sum
Of foliage, branches and seed.

Whatever your particular bent
Nature calls out to everyone,
I sure am happy that I went
Walking and gathering words for fun.

Moving to the Country

There are many verses
Written about noises
In my back yard besides voices.

Birds, squirrels and bees
But what's not talked about by me
Are lawnmowers and automobiles.

Ignore them, I hear you say
But obsessive attention will play
And not let me rest today.

I'm moving out, really
Out to the country
To a ten acre prairie.

Where animals and birds
Will be my friends
Bringing me joy to the end.

You will get bored, I hear you say
Maybe I will but today
That's my plan come what may.

Love Lives Here
Ekphrastic poem (art-inspired words)
Painting, Farm in Winter by Kathy Blankenheim

White on white
Brown on blue
Winter colors layered on canvas.

Who came before?
Who lives there now
Keeping tradition alive?

I can hear rumblings from my past,
Tin cups rattling against
Scattered stained plates of Delphware.

Square wooden boxes
Instead of chairs
Set about the fireplace.

Praying on knees
Sore from pressing down, hands clasped,
Face pointed toward the ceiling.

Quick peep outside
Through lace curtains, grey with dust.
Darkness echoic of humdrum sound.

Wintertime is only one season
Long and cold with some relief
Giving us hope for warmer days.

Shadows spreading out from trees
Laid bare by wind and rain
Over time, spring will come.

The hidden animals will surface
Humans will speed up their pace
Across the snowy, muddy path.

Laughter will be heard again
Doorbell chime ringing
From visitors with apple pie.

This house, this farm waits
For change that leads to future bliss
Whether executed or extinguished

The house stays or dilapidates
Never to be abandoned,
Love lives here.

Barn Door

Red barn, symbol of home,
Land and lake, my destiny.
No matter where I roam,
It comes back to serenity.
Path leading to open door,
Symbol of friendliness.
Whether rich or poor,
I can be happy, I guess.
Red barn, feeling of comfort,
Standing at the end of the path.
For a moment, I feel no hurt,
At last peace has conquered wrath.

Loving Where I am Planted
Carmel, Indiana

I am riveted by Carmel, from ordinary to extraordinary,
The designs are new and old, simple and complicated,
Observing from top of city center, I tarry
To take in the farmers market spread
Fresh with produce, craft and taffy.

Festivals of art, stories and song
Together, bring about economic and community growth
Blending cultures from Cork, Ireland to Hong Kong
The arts and design elements both
Combine to make our city strong.

The manicured landscapes of the roundabout leads
The way to color and symmetry of a suburban future
Unique to urban living, a choice of city or rural meets my needs
The Monon with its active lifestyle cuts a path through nature
Where a large white egret lands and feeds.

The Palladium and theatre location
Short distance from Main Street
Speaks to Mayor Brainard's lofty vision
A man, who upon seeing you will meet and greet
With warm attention to your conversation.

Around the traditional well where water is drawn
You can see people interact with pleasure
Life here is comfortable and through giving a helping hand
I cherish the opportunity to be myself and nurture
My talents, planted here on the city land.

Zionsville: A Sense of Place

A house stayed on the housing market
Six months and waiting
I showed up ten minutes before
Open house closed
Stepped in and that was that...

Symmetry, balance, old world charm
Reminded me of home, a space,
A place and time captured in memory
And now the memory becomes a new reality.

Maple trees on Maple Street,
Hydrangeas to the left while sitting on my porch.
The brick drive that looks like art after rain,
But oh! In Summer, weeds and moss
Causing me to sigh before beautifying again.

Long walks through leafy lane ways
Between houses loved and worn by generations.
Shopping for art, jewelry and clothes,
Window displays that mirror lives of passersby.

Restaurants; American, Italian, and French,
Conversation and coffee at Roasted in the Village
From smell of Guatemalan coffee to Earl Grey tea.
Black Dog Books, with beautiful new and rare books,
Invites you to take a seat on the front porch bench.

Saturdays in summertime are synonymous
With Farmer's Market for over twenty-five years
Thanks to the brainchild of Barb Munson.

And Sullivan Munce Cultural Center
With its past and present relevance
Hosts Poetry on Brick Street, first Thursdays
Reminding us of service to the community.

Zionsville Chamber of Commerce and Boone EDC
People of vision and leadership
Extending friendship and support
To people and businesses like me.

A list of all things familiar,
Walking around Elm Green
Onwards toward Zionsville Lions Club Park,
Trees lining roads and river,
People fishing in ripples.
Birds chirping and dogs barking,
Cars vrooming by and by,
Grass cutting, house remodeling,
Sounds that soothe and some that annoy.

And now a place of my own.
A place to sit by the fire in winter,
A swing removed to make way for extra seating,
A meeting place, a laughing place,
A watching-the-world-go-by place.

The Willow Street sign that signifies a bend
From that old dream "the willow tree will be in the first round"
A sign, figuratively says, "Welcome Home"
You have found your sense of place.

ii

people

Little Girl
*Ekphrastic poem from the painting by Marie Goth,
on display at Brown County Art Guild, Indiana*

Little girl, what is your mood?
Sensing bond of love,
Between viewer and the viewed
Little doll, inanimate appendage
Together, living a life of privilege.

Capturing spirit and time
The painter moves us to her world.
Passion and art combine
Brush strokes set the stage for dialogue
Stirring mystery like a fog.

Living, breathing, loving girl
Your destiny yet to unfold
Like an oyster making a pearl
Life's treasures inherited and experienced
Stuck in time, forever present.

Little girl, what is your mood?

Patchwork Quilter
Ekphrastic poem from the painting by Marie Goth,
on display at Brown County Art Guild, Indiana

Patchwork quilter, maker of life and love
Hours of devotion to her craft above.
Sitting for the artist's skillful pleasure
Like a poet weaving words on a page for leisure.

What keeps you busy all day long?
What makes the stitches' rhythmic song?
When will you complete this endeavor?
Will you keep on creating forever?

Sowing and stitching over and over
Someday, to someone else, this quilt will transfer.
For now, the rush of higher calling than material things
Brings about tiredness that aches until the ache zings.

For me, the poet, the style of clothes has changed
The spinning wheel spins silk threads of words instead.
Like this woman, I too show pain and pleasure on my face
I too have my shoulders wrapped in lace.

So, the quilter, artist and I are bound
Through this engaging gaze found
In this artist's portrait and now my poem
About a patchwork quilt and a creative woman.

Wedding Day
James and Lindsay

Today, a day to savor in your heart,
Smiles from ear to ear, oh! glorious start,
Forever and a day, may love be sweet.
Laughter and fortune showered at your feet.
Friends uplifting should problems arise,
Family to be there for lows and highs.
On this wedding day, a beautiful bride
Meets a gallant groom with unflinching pride.
Blessings bestowed, fond memories unfold,
Candles shimmer, two rings glimmer with gold.
These words will help you whether night or day
Catch them as they flutter and float your way.
Forever and always, kindness is key
Love and happiness will light your journey.

Aubrey Lynn from Nana

Aubrey, I love you,
Most wanted and loved
You belong to the earth.
Because of your love, everything is possible.

You touched my heart
You made me feel
I loved you as soon as I heard your name.

Walk with me and share a path to destiny
You are not alone.
Together with family
Life will be full and exciting
Forever will be.

Harper Katherine from Nana

The day came and then the night turned to morn
Into this new world where you brought the light.
I rejoiced when I heard that you were born
Picture of health and beautiful sight.

Connected to your mother and father
Known only through a photograph, I heart
Your name, repeated over and over,
Connected and curious from the start.

Sleep well and stay strong, until we will meet
Tomorrow, the perfect get together,
I want to count your fingers and greet
And tell how I will love you forever.

The first meeting was beautiful
I felt you move and kick
While you nestled in my arm,
No fuss, comforted and comforting,
Breathing, sleeping peacefully.

Long legged and long fingered
You pursed your lips to drink.
Along with both sets of grandparents,
New parents, proud and devoted,
Hovered, beaming excitedly.

Rays of hope can shine again
As if to say, "I'm here,
I've come for a reason"
Laughter and shared pleasure,
Time for happiness and joy.

You've change the world by your shining entrance,
I want to see you take the stage and dance.

Chloe Elizabeth from Nana

This time with your name on our lips
Chloe, we waited patiently
All the while ready to do jumping jacks and flips.
We heard you were resting quietly.

Waiting, waiting for your birth
Each minute ticked by slowly
Then with excited breath,
Eight pounds, twelve ounces only!

You are here now, skin like silk
Beautiful girl, beautiful soul too,
Close your eyes and drink your milk
Till tomorrow, may sleep come over you.

The day after has come, now the waiting is over
Bringing joy and peaceful aura
I anticipate your touch and scent like a flower
Counting the hours till I see my "little Indiana."

This poem must pause for a time
I'll be back to tell the story with laughter
Of how I felt and what I saw and another rhyme
To describe the meeting of a new granddaughter.

I'm back, it felt surreal
What I saw was love and peace
Parents living with zeal
Blessings will never cease.

A family united, a special bond
I couldn't be happier to witness
This picture perfect scenario beyond
Anticipation, beyond joyousness.

The here and now forever
The now and here together.

Sophie Jane from Nana

Everything feels right
The right time to be
Loving parents will show you the light
So fortunate to be born in twenty twenty-three.

I long to see you and love you forever
I long to know you and be your support
Your cousins ready to play together
First cousins, second cousins will want to cavort.

Irish blood through and through
Passing to you from generations
Looking forward to nurturing you
While you learn the traditions.

A girl! a girl! a girl!!!
That's one very lucky baby
Counting the days to give you a whirl
A joy to behold, a joy to see.

Counting weeks, minutes and seconds
Coming home to Indiana
What an amazing journey beckons
What a thrill, maybe a ballerina?

A singer, a musician, a writer
Whatever your heart desires
A doctor, an attorney, a farmer
Plenty of choices to light your fires.

Your name Sophie Jane suits you
Born on Thanksgiving night
Beautiful baby at three hours, first view,
Tomorrow, I will hold you tight.

What an amazing journey beckons
Loving parents will show you the light.

Very Proud Nana

My granddaughter, Harper, who is three,
Spoke to me on the phone on Saturday evening.
Her voice delivered what to me sounded like a poem.
She said:
Nana,
I want to tell you something.
We are going to Conner Prairie tomorrow
And we are going to have breakfast.
First
She addresses me Nana.
She's setting me up for a communication.
Second
I want to tell you something
She has a message.
Third
I want to tell you
She's clear on identifying her audience.
Fourth
We are going
We, she's making a connection.
Fifth
To Conner Prairie
The name of a place that conjures up history,
Openness to truth, respect and lessons learned.
Sixth
And, use of word and – conjunction
And is a coordinating conjunction –
A coordinating conjunction connects
Words, phrases, and clauses of equal importance.
And there's more! More anticipation!
Seventh
We are going to have
Hope for the future.
Eight
Breakfast
Food!! My favorite meal….
Another connection,
Communion with the senses.
Now I hope you can see why I said her words were like a poem.

Reflection of a Perfect Visit

Where have you been?
I haven't been anywhere since last seen.
I'm sorry. Its been a little crazy.
The child ponders and looks at me quizzically!

I show up and love flows
A beautiful emotion knows
A connection, a family commitment
Where time is an important element.

An open, smiling grin greets me
Hand in hand we go where food is key
With stomachs full, we are ready to chatter
About Taylor Swift, Ed Sheeran and Hozier.

Music leads us to our shared dance fest
Half an inch in growth on the chart since last visit
Division and multiplication are practiced and known
Shoes tossed, socks off, a feeling of home.

Back again, road seems short, filled with music and song
A hug, a smile, a knowing that another visit will come.
Simple and beautiful bond,
Till next time, love is strong.

On Seeing a Woman's Side Profile
In likeness of my mother

"Unbelievable", sums it up
To see someone so like, in outline,
The nose, the mouth, the color of the hair
The facial movements, I had forgotten.

What does it mean? Why now?
What timing made me choose
To enter the hairdresser's that day, that hour?
Memories choked me with emotion.

My mother's image, a woman named Gerry
She must have thought me strange to ask
But she'd have known, I was compelled to approach
The pull was strong, I had to question.

Unpack the memories,
Unpack the emotion
And know the reason was to compose
This poem of devotion.

Hands

From glorious smooth hands
"Piano hands" they used to say
I look down and see the wrinkled knuckles,
And feel the arthritic pain of spur and cyst.

Nails are manicured and rings displayed
Finding beauty in color and sparkle
My world brightens and shines
Focusing on joy in every handshake.

These hands held babies
Raised high in cheer and pleasure
The same hands have comforted grown men,
Now they type words of reflection.

Beautiful hands, beautiful time
Reaching out is an everlasting gift.

iii

gratitude

A Moment in Time

The time is now to open your eyes,
Let light in, let anger out
Complex compilation of lies,
Built up tension, makes me want to shout.

Just like snow covers the ground
Frozen in time contains the pain,
A new shape, a new meaning is found
Encapsulating grief, it drips like rain.

Begin again, muddied
With each ebb and flow a clearer me
The suffering soul is freed
A new lock, a new key.

Gratitude for Life and Love
Parents married 27 November,1947, Mother's birthday

A vow to love, a wish to be loved
The giver and the receiver both
Connected and betrothed on a special day.

Facing the future, so sure and steady
To be rocked by and tested over time
Ever ready to be strong.

A force of good, a desire to be great
Dignified in life and death
They were my world.

The gift of love keeps giving
Their blood, now my blood
Their strength, now my strength.

That special day, a birthday and a wedding
Gave rise to my creation.

Lessons in Life

Who knows where the lessons come from?
Why they come?
When they come?
What are they meant to teach us?

These questions popped in my head
Just like the lessons themselves without warning.
I stopped the car to write these thoughts down
No immediate answers came, just repetitive words.

They come
They come in the early hours of the morning
They come at night.
They come to soothe and they come to disrupt.

Lessons in life come for you and me always
Let the dust settle and start over.
And then an answer came
Lessons come to teach us grace and gratitude for breath.

Passage of Time

Clear demarcation of sand, sea and sky
Like passages of time
Some spaces represent low and high
Some phases have no reason or rhyme.

Stubborn like the line drawn in the sand
No room for scorn
Balance of power in hand
Command presence is born.

Time to reflect, time to select
New beginnings, fresh to start
Distance helps to detect
Those who feel with their heart.

Thank You, Grandma
My Mom

I found a penny today
And raised it toward the sky with
My usual gratitude, "thanks grandma"
My Mom, grandma to my two boys.

She wrote a letter for each before
Her dementia set in fully
Knowing that she was leaving
Something concrete for them to hold.

Her handwriting neat and cursive
Words equally spaced,
Her index finger and thumb clenched
To hold the plastic pen.

The beginning, "My Dearest"
She stops, contemplating what to say.
Sitting beside a coal fire with sticks crackling.
In juxtaposition, her silent visualization.

Next, a frown, a smile, a darting eye
Intent on getting each word onto the page.
Leaning forward, her perfume spilling into the air
Mixing with smoke from the fire.

She quietly writes a few sentences.
Intermittently, she looks fondly on photos on her mantle
Framed photos of grandchildren smiling back at her
She too smiles and goes back to writing.

Each letter uniquely crafted
Holding a special meaning for each of my boys
Both equal and similar in opening and closing signature
She comes to an end,
All my love From Grandma xxxxxx

iv

contemplation

Simple Rejection

"Sorry, I have to tell you that you did not make it.
Your art is simple."
I say, "Thank you for your phone call."

It felt like slings and arrows were hurled at me.
Internalized pain burst inside
And then infected my soul.
My loss encapsulated with feelings of grief and anger.
My words came fast and furious
Decisions by narrow-minded people are always bad decisions.

Dictionary in hand,
I sought to understand.
How subjective is art?
When is simple a bad thing?
Conceptualism is complex and simple.
Art can be simple, simply perfect or imperfect.

Days passed and weeks passed.
Often, I think on what might have been
I would have fitted in! I am good enough!
My body walks by the gallery with quick steps
My eyes pointed away for the most part
And still, a small piece of me wants to peer inside.

This door closed, another opened.
My dignity is intact.
I say, art is art, simple or not.

Another Rejection

This time it hurts but not as bad.
With slowed down response, being prepared helps
Breath in, deep breath out with pursed lips!

Headlines could read:
Rebel from rebel county takes a beating.
Down but not out, out but not down!

Light bulb moment coming on!
No that was a flashing light from the kettle
Time for tea. Time for happy face and thick skin!

Cork, Ireland is known as The Rebel County

Café Life

Sitting and reflecting on the comings and goings
Chit chat, reflections on past days,
Snippets of conversations infused with smell of coffee.

Life looks great from the high top table
Time to sit, time to view.

Music all around, Sinatra at his best
Singing along in my head and nodding
Like old times, repeat, repeat, repeat.

Life looks great from the high top table
Time to sit, time to view.

The hope of release of stress
Sometimes it happens, sometimes it doesn't.
Wonderful day or not.

Life looks great from the high top table
Time to sit, time to view.

Oasis away from oasis
Friends drop by and chat and drink
Today, tomorrow, anticipation is the only thing guaranteed.

Life looks great from the high top table
Time to sit, time to view.

Waiting

With pen in hand, I turn to Constable for inspiration
The great painter of clouds, sky
And landscape of a local nature
John, a miller's son, defied his father's profession
And chose to contemplate, feel and paint

This poet, fatherless for thirty-seven years
With no one to defy
In fact, I am well supported
Even encouraged

So, why the need to look for inspiration?
Why write if nothing moves me?
Why sing when out of tune?

Constable looked at paintings non-traditionally
Others revered tradition and chose imitation

I wait in silence for my next poem

writing

my next poem arrived in time to save me
troubled with anxiety and doubt
it came to soothe and calm my inner self
two steps forward and three back
awake again to color and sound
vibrations of tingling
half pain, half pleasure to be writing
earnest search for words
they come with consonants and vowels
a sequence of sounds built up with rhythm
the capitalized beginnings gone
replaced with closer to the ground letters
serving the same purpose to communicate
line by line, verse by verse
repetition being a part of the hypnotizing beat
hammering home the sound of silence
alliteration finding its own effect to emphasize
how special language is and how words can fill your mind
along with onomatopoeia and rhyme, the words spill and thrill
these new poems are newly crafted
the hope is to bring a fresh spirit and find a space, a headspace
from which to make a difference.

Glass Paperweight

Someone crafted me and let me go
Separated from my maker, I stand strong
Like a glass paperweight
Hiding a dead weight from the world.
Looks can be deceiving,
Airy and aerated with bubbles
Sitting pretty, looking fragile
All the time tasked to hold down
Whatever is capable of flying
Off in many directions.
You can call me wife, mother, grandmother,
Sister, aunt or friend,
Relationships seen through the prism of life,
Transparent and honest, made with love
In the end, calm and beauty win.

You Are Your Own Kite

Something needs to happen to stir the muse,
Some thought, some emotion must light the fuse.
From hilltop view to valley deep
A bird, a goat, a woolly sheep,
An action or a metaphor takes place
Fly high, soar low, 'you are your own kite' in this case.

The string is pulled, the west wind wilts
The uplift of the fabric tilts.
Like life the ups are short
The downs take time to sort.
The kite, you, can adjust
Rising again, to shake the dust.

The wind, string and kite
Are tugged along by might.
The poem also has a motion
A spell bound message, in the form of a potion.
After setting the scene
I hope you understand what I mean.

Words Come in Dreams

"Anchor Hill" was one of those phrases
Showed up in the night.
Not knowing where it came from
Or where it was going,
I wrote it down.

Last time that happened was "Willow Trees"
Followed by seeing willow trees.
Anchor Hill sounds like a steep climb,
Uphill struggle grounded
With strong pull to save the day.

I like when words come to me in my sleep.
It stirs my curiosity,
Wakes my imagination,
Makes me look for messages
And gives me access to another world.

Through the Window

Close my eyes, what do I see?
Circular view through the window.
Translucent waves wander inwards freely
Like life, they ebb and flow.

Open my eyes, where am I?
Two worlds collide and fade.
I'm here, I'm there, I'm low, I'm high,
Like art wonderfully made.

Words and images transport me
Through the window to the soul.
This is what I know, this is what I see,
Accepting me for me, makes me whole.

Before the Rain and Then

Hidden sunlight befriends the rain clouds
Forming and growing more dense
At its heaviest, I admire its beauty

Bunnies cease chasing each other
Birds continue to chirp, not a stir of wind yet
Squirrels gnaw down nuts for protein

Rain starts, a tap, a repetitive tap
And then nothing, as if to tease me
Short intermittent taps, an ominous sound

Bang, crash, thunder clapping from afar
The electric lights dance on and off
Darkness shifts, I see an emblazoned sky

Now, even I scurry to get inside
Away from windows, into the belly of the house
Until everything returns to before the rain

And then, safe to step outside,
My interrupted life gets back to normal, new normal
Until the next rain disrupts my outside slumber.

Hand Written Letter

A letter came and cheered me
Old fashioned pen and paper sent
Poem dissected, and enjoyed
Unexpected praise, unsolicited comments
One person took the time to notice.

At a different stage of life
That letter might have come too late
But patience is a beautiful thing
Giving up is not an option
Who will listen? Who will read?
Until my last breath, shall breathe no more.

The Torn Letter

When you write a letter
That says all you have to say
And tear it up
You feel a sense of relief.

Words are strewn on the page,
You look at the cracks
Where the words got separated
And feel the pain.

Better to feel from here
Writing your poems
Than to deliver the truth of your pain.
At least for now.

You go about your life
Taking care of those in close proximity
Knowing that right is right
And right doesn't always make you happy.

Hanging Pear

Pear suspended in air,
Beauty at its best,
Dimpled cheek,
Hourglass shape,
She brightens the dark.

Hovering, hanging in space,
Silent, strong and stark,
All alone and complete.

Red Bowl

Special shaped bowl
Full of fruit
Vibrant, sweet aroma overflowing.

Bent, not broken
Willowing, bouncing back,
Thick skinned and bruised
Yellow bananas at their peak.

Connected and bunched
Shiny and glowing,
Pick me, I am good for you.

She Gave Me Courage

Already instilled with hope,
She gave me courage,
Another phone call, another woman of strength.
This time her name is Nancy Baxter
An author, publisher and coach.
Nancy's generosity of time and talent
Bestowed on me a confidence to grow.
A continuance of being mothered,
The sense of wisdom and history,
Of passing on jewels filled with light and color.
Her guidance and voice distinctive and unique
Now, on this side of the ocean, my trilogy complete
I'm excited to get out and shout
"Find a mentor" and in turn give homage by
Shining and being a beacon of hope
and courage for others.

Let Prayer Win – Looking for a Miracle

You probably have heard these words
He's young, he's fit, he gets his strength from you
Prayers sent and simple "thank you" texted back.
A bridge between silence and pain
A rope of hope thrown to a frantic mother
Worst nightmare doesn't come close
And yet, life is amazing.
Who stays, who leaves, who knows,
Whether young or old, whether fit or not
The doctors' and nurses' skills matter
The intuition of what works, what doesn't work
Direction from mentors and scholars
Modern medical science knowledge along with
Channeling energy and pure positive vibes
Pass into and out of a young man's brain.
Don't give up, don't give in
I have seen prayer work, I believe prayer will win.

Eames Table and Chair
Ekphrastic poem, Painting,
Eames Table and Chair *by Amanda W. Mathis*

Standing still in time
This view of a room
Shines a spotlight on legacy.

The vibe, color and positioning
Though probably happenstance
Tells a story.

A story of era,
A story of comfort,
A story of quality.

How do I relate?
Seeing defined outlines
Gives me a sense of structure.

A sense of order,
A sense of color combinations
With a punctuation of purple.

Outlining whimsical cat,
Geometric shapes, chairs and table
Draw me into this capsule of time.

Forever staged, signs of wear and tear on the rug
A reminder of the fragility of life.
This painting will live longer than me.

For now, a sense of occupying
A personal space and the artist's space
Makes me feel complete.

Finding Purple

At a workshop by Lani O'Hanlon,
She asked us to think of an herb.
I thought of lavender and its color purple.
That same day, in the middle of my parent's grave
I found a purple stone.

I touched it. A shiny, marble-like stone
It wasn't mine so I left it there.
No other graves had purple colored stones.
There was one with shiny white and silver like stones
But no purple!

Sitting in a restaurant on that same day,
I looked down. The carpet was purple!
Goat cheese with purple beetroot for dinner.
Do you see a pattern or a trend?
Can you see purple?

My antennae are up. This time the word purple
Jumped out at me from an essay by Tom McCarthy.
My name in purple on my forthcoming book
Designed by Nicolas Sanquest
Who didn't know about the purple story!

I received an email
Asking for my books to be sent for review.
I was invited to read my original poem
As part of the creative interlude at a Zionsville TedX talk.
I have been most fortunate since seeing the purple stone.

The memory of seeing the stone brings comfort and joy
A clear picture captured in my mind.
I will visit the grave again,
Picking up the purple stone if it is still there.
No matter what, I am my own purple stone.

Lessons From Your Best Self

Move gently to and fro
Like the beats of a metronome on slow tempo.
Visualize the purple and yellow wild flowers
Blooming annually.

Remember the old stream that trickles down the hill
Let it cleanse and swish the pain around
Like the saliva in your mouth
Protects you from lingering bacteria.

If your heart shatters into pieces,
Too sharp and dangerous to carry,
Hunker down for the long haul of winter
And bounce back like the flowers of spring.

Once Again

Caw-caw, tweet-tweet
Constant communication
Clicking in my ears
And then the thunder roared.

A sense of foreboding destiny
Aligned with heavy gloom,
Nature's high and low sounds
Reflecting the extremes of possibility.

Pitter-patter of rain drops begin
Followed by the grasses' aroma intensifying,
Swaying branches make loud
Swooshing sounds of leaves.

And then, heaviness in the air subsiding,
The light breeze brings freshness,
Birds and squirrels chatter, unseen,
Returned, birds chase each other.

With Purple in Sight

The effect of purple shows itself
Through depth and density of color,
As a splash and dash of paint
It elicits a sense of fluidity.

Hills, vales, heat haze and flowers,
Everything that pulses saturated purple
Gives me strength, connection,
Lesson and breakthrough.

Staying strong is necessary to being heard
Connecting to intention helps with being honest.
The lesson is out there
And the breakthrough will reveal itself.

With purple in sight, before, behind
To the sides and betwixt
The outcome is uncertain
But in time, destiny awaits.

Dancing Flowers

Let loose, let go
Swing high, swing low,
Wild flowers dance
What do you see at first glance?

Busy lines emitting energy
Giving out sparks of electricity,
Like an onion shedding its peel
How does it make you feel?

Take a risk, take a chance
Get ready to dance,
Live your life without fear
Step up and give a loud cheer!